Spelling Six

An Interactive Vocabulary & Spelling Workbook for 10 & 11-Year-Olds.

(With AudioBook Lessons)

By
Bukky Ekine-Ogunlana

www.tcecpublishing.com

© Copyright Bukky Ekine-Ogunlana 2024 – All rights reserved.

The content of this book may not be reproduced, duplicated, or transmitted without direct written permission from the author or the publisher. Under no circumstance will any blame or legal responsibility be held against the publisher, or author, for any damages, reparation, or monetary loss due to the information contained within this book. Either directly or indirectly. You are responsible for your own choices, actions, and results.

Legal Notice:
This book is copyright protected. This book is only for personal use. You cannot amend, distribute, sell, use, quote, or paraphrase any part, or the content within this book, without the consent of the author or publisher.

Disclaimer Notice:
Please note the information contained within this document is for educational and entertainment purposes only. All effort has been executed to present accurate, up-to-date, reliable, and complete information. No warranties of any kind are declared or implied. Readers acknowledge that the author is not engaging in the rendering of legal, financial, medical, or professional advice. The content within this book has been derived from various sources. Please consult a licensed professional before attempting any techniques outlined in this book.

By reading this document, the reader agrees that under no circumstances is the author responsible for any direct or indirect losses incurred as a result of the use of the information contained within this document, including, but not limited to, errors, omissions, or inaccuracies.

Published by
TCEC Publishing

Table of Contents

Dedication 6
Introduction 7

Spelling 6 - 1 8
Spelling 6 - 2 12
Spelling 6 - 3 16
Spelling 6 - 4 20
Spelling 6 - 5 24
Spelling 6 - 6 28
Spelling 6 - 7 32
Spelling 6 - 8 36
Spelling 6 - 9 40
Spelling 6 - 10 44
Spelling 6 - 11 48
Spelling 6 - 12 52
Spelling 6 - 13 56
Spelling 6 - 14 60
Spelling 6 - 15 64
Spelling 6 - 16 68
Spelling 6 - 17 72
Spelling 6 - 18 76
Spelling 6 - 19 80
Spelling 6 - 20 84

Table of Contents

Spelling 6 - 21 88
Spelling 6 - 22 92
Spelling 6 - 23 96
Spelling 6 - 24 100
Spelling 6 - 25 104

Conclusion..107
Answers..131
Other Books You'll Love! 146
Audiobook..150
Facebook Community 152
References 153

Dedication

This book is dedicated to our three exceptional children and all the beautiful children worldwide who have passed through the T.C.E.C 6-16 years programme over the years. Thank you for the opportunity to serve you and invest in your colourful and bright future.

Introduction

Welcome to the sixth book of the Spelling for Kids series. Spelling six has 300 new words in store for you. It is ideal for ten-to-eleven-year-olds.

Three hundred new words will be added to your vocabulary to improve your spelling skills.

Prepare yourself for that spelling gold medal. You are almost there! Undoubtedly, by now, your listening skills and your memory have improved, and you are capable of writing correctly about 1,700 words!

You can continue in the sixth book to raise your score. And if you want, ask your parents to help you keep score.

Let's get rolling! Time is precious!

Spelling 6-1

1. Spell:
Freddy was asked to _____ his work on Thursday but he handed it in on Friday.

2. Spell:
The girls were _____ to know the winner of the dance competition.

3. Spell:
Diana has a good sense of _____.

Spelling 6-1

4. Spell:

Lola paid her _____ bill early and earned a discount.

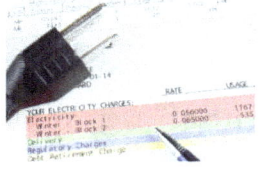

5. Spell:

Damien wrote a _____ on Nelson Mandela.

6. Spell:

The groom's friends will throw a _____ party for him before the wedding.

Spelling 6-1

7. Spell:
Tim has been complaining of tummy _____ since morning.

8. Spell:
I will _____ in the school play.

9. Spell:
The accountant detected _____ activity on his account and called him to alert the bank.

Spelling 6-1

10. Spell:

Paul pulled a _____ when he went to the gym for his weekly exercise.

11. Spell:

The _____ party won the last election.

12. Spell:

The judge should _____ the thief for the theft.

> Congrats! You have finished learning the words in lesson 1. Remember to know and understand the meaning of all the new words you have found.

Spelling 6-2

1. Spell:

The judge discharged him as not

_____.

2. Spell:

The medicine was able to cure the

_____ completely.

3. Spell:

It did not _____ to Dan to

wake Lucy up at 7 am, so she

slept and missed her bus.

Spelling 6-2

4. Spell:

Mathew has made the payment with his _____card.

5. Spell:

The latest keyboard is _____ in performance to the older ones.

6. Spell:

Bella loves to _____ her mum in her room.

Spelling 6-2

7. Spell:

Ryan had a prolific _____ with the headteacher about improving the school.

8. Spell:

Sienna spent thirty minutes sitting on a _____ bike.

9. Spell:

The trophy stood on a _____.

Spelling 6-2

10. Spell:

Ben is _____ and numerate.

11. Spell:

The story going around is a

_____ and not

at all true.

12. Spell:

The class performance was a brilliant

_____ for the

school.

Well done! You have finished learning the words in lesson 2.

Spelling 6-3

1. Spell:

The _____ on the investment was 20 percent.

2. Spell:

Scott has a strong _____ to help and care for his grandparents.

3. Spell:

John was not elected as the _____ so he would return to work.

Spelling 6-3

4. Spell:

There will be a maths lesson in the last

_____ today.

5. Spell:

Aliya sat at the _____ end

of the class because she was

sad.

6. Spell:

Cox speaks four different

_____ languages

confidently.

Spelling 6-3

7. Spell:
Rose had to correct all the _____ words and mark them with a green pen.

8. Spell:
It works better to ask someone to do something than to _____ him to do it.

9. Spell:
Greg lives with his dad, and he has remained under his _____.

Spelling 6-3

10. Spell:
Tracey traveled to Texas to get a decent

_____ in a private

college.

11. Spell:
Freddie's shirt is smaller in

_____ with his dad's

12. Spell:
Mr. Marcus is close to _____

up a deal with the new company.

You've made it! You completed lesson 3. Pay attention, kids; if you find it difficult to learn some words, you should write them down on paper. That will help you remember better.

Spelling 6-4

1. Spell:

The Christmas dinner was

_ .

2. Spell:

Trees _ _ _ _ _ _ _ _ _ _ _ _ _ _ _ _ _ _ _ the garden.

3. Spell:

Lisa used the _ _ _ _ _ _ _ _ _ _ _ _ _ _ _ _ _ _ _ stove to

do her cooking.

Spelling 6-4

4. Spell:

The _____ center is going to be closed for the weekend.

5. Spell:

The doctor had an _____ call, so he went to attend to it.

6. Spell:

I wish I could be _____ for one day, so I could hear what others say about me.

Spelling 6-4

7. Spell:

The shoemaker was asked to _____ the cost he had charged for repairing the shoes.

8. Spell:

The _____ was not opened today because of the public holiday.

9. Spell:

Nancy did _____ her savings because she was spending a lot on Christmas gifts.

Spelling 6-4

10. Spell:

The _____ came to the house to unplug the drain.

11. Spell:

The _____ happens twice a year when the day and the night are of equal length.

12. Spell:

Teddy was watching out for the _____ when he was driving.

Great! Lesson 4 is over!

Spelling 6-5

1. Spell:
A _____ is one or more letters added to the end of a sentence.

2. Spell:
The _____ of the city have deserted it because of the war.

3. Spell:
Mary earns a _____ job salary and can afford a big house.

Spelling 6-5

4. Spell:

The bride walked with her father down the

_____ joyfully.

5. Spell:

_____ lives are lost during

the war.

6. Spell:

Jessica has shown a _____

interest in maths.

Spelling 6-5

7. Spell:

The servants _____ the king by taking a bow.

8. Spell:

Blake has decided to _____ a career in piloting.

9. Spell:

Harrold did not _____ he was loud when he was giving his explanation on global warming.

Spelling 6-5

10. Spell:

Mom uses the _____ cleaner to clean the floor.

11. Spell:

Hilda is in _____ pain as a result of the accident.

12. Spell:

There was no _____ for Michelle's sister to stay with her in the hospital, though she wanted to.

Lesson 5 is over! Great work!

Spelling 6-6

1. Spell:

Riley has made _____ and progressive improvements in his spelling by doing it every Friday.

2. Spell:

Clarke enjoys playing _____ with Elli-May at the sports club.

3. Spell:

Robert stopped to help the firefighters when he saw the _____ building.

Spelling 6-6

4. Spell:

The troops invaded the foreign country's

_____.

5. Spell:

Experiments in class help us understand

better the _____

of physics.

6. Spell:

Ukraine is under a terrible

_____ by the

Russian army.

Spelling 6-6

7. Spell:
Bradly did _____ to the left while playing football, then to the right.

8. Spell:
Only a _____ of the students bring their lunch packs to school.

9. Spell:
Ronnie went to _____ ten percent of the money required when ordering a cake.

Spelling 6-6

10. Spell:

Lennon was utterly _____ of the game's rules, so he shoved all the other boys.

11. Spell:

Leon's explanation was not _____ for not completing his homework, so he did not get playtime.

12. Spell:

The news was spreading in the northern _____ of the country.

Great! Lesson 6 is over! I suggest you get some rest before going on to the next lesson. That will help you recharge and return to the next task more refreshed! Great work!

Spelling 6-7

1. Spell:

The patient's _____ deteriorated after leaving the hospital.

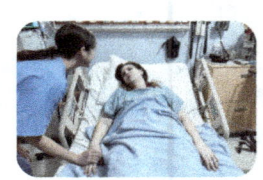

2. Spell:

Christopher was staring at the _____ in the exam hall because he did not know the answers.

3. Spell:

Kevin and Ethan joined the bigger _____ to play with more innovative players.

Spelling 6-7

4. Spell:

The chocolate factory will

_____ to produce

mini chocolates from September.

5. Spell:

Sami made a _____ to get

attention.

6. Spell:

Hilda's fuel _____ was full,

so she did not need to buy more

petrol for her car.

Spelling 6-7

7. Spell:

Riley could not _____ his reasons for coming late to the P.E class.

8. Spell:

The _____ will be completely closed in the summer.

9. Spell:

Benjamin wrote an interesting _____ about his immediate family.

Spelling 6-7

10. Spell:

No one could _____ Evie after her face paint.

11. Spell:

Vinny's anger rose at Asif's _____ words because he felt insulted.

12. Spell:

Mr. Hunt found a _____ of truth in Joan's explanations.

Fantastic! You have finished the words in lesson 7. What a task! Kids, keep a note: An easy way to learn the majority of new words is to break them apart; in that way, the words can be easily organized from the shortest to the longest.

Spelling 6-8

1. Spell:

Alexander and Vinny _____ each other, so they do not talk.

2. Spell:

Mercy is a terrible _____ on her friends to do what she wants.

3. Spell:

The charity gave some food to the families that were in _____ because of famine.

Spelling 6-8

4. Spell:
Danny planned to _____ his dad, but he was caught.

5. Spell:
The doctor put an _____ bandage around Tina's palm.

6. Spell:
_____ screens separated the hall.

Spelling 6-8

7. Spell:

On _____ , he makes a profit of about $1,000 a month by selling ice cream.

8. Spell:

The _____ artist is coming for the sports day.

9. Spell:

Rob has his _____ plans for the next elections.

Spelling 6-8

10. Spell:

Kevin used a _____ marker to write his name on his water bottle.

11. Spell:

The team leader came to _____ everyone who supported the team.

12. Spell:

The _____ date for the elections is the 12th of November.

Look at you! You are doing so well! And it seems that you will be a spelling bee master pretty soon! You have just finished lesson 8.

Spelling 6-9

1. Spell:
Tina met an _____ guy that enjoys doing extreme sports.

2. Spell:
Emily allowed her_____ to run wild.

3. Spell:
Dora listened to an ancient _____, and she found it fascinating.

Spelling 6-9

4. Spell:
The _____ piece of land could not produce any fruit after several attempts.

5. Spell:
Mr. Mark yelled at the _____ trainee since he constantly made noise.

6. Spell:
Anna will be singing _____ in the new choir.

Spelling 6-9

7. Spell:

An expensive colorful _____ arrived at Amelia's table on Monday from an unknown admirer.

8. Spell:

Mom uses the porcelain dinnerware only on a special _____.

9. Spell:

Ronaldo will be working in the _____ company after his graduation.

Spelling 6-9

10. Spell:

Robison was in good _____ today and thus made us laugh a lot.

11. Spell:

Lawrence was determined to finish reading the _____ book before having his meal.

12. Spell:

Mr. Porter is a _____ visitor to the school's community library.

Well done! You have finished lesson C. You should be proud of yourself. And remember this: Always enunciate each word properly; this method will help you spell the word correctly.

Spelling 6-10

1. Spell:

Derek deserves an _____ from Emily for being rude to him.

2. Spell:

Debby kept the food in the freezer to help _____ it.

3. Spell:

The _____ stood at attention in front of his boss and saluted.

Spelling 6-10

4. Spell:
He read out his _____ story, and it was exemplary.

5. Spell:
The house had _____ and calmness after the three sisters settled their grievances.

6. Spell:
Anita helped Abigail with the meal _____ for their dinner.

Spelling 6-10

7. Spell:

Cole was wise to have saved his

_____ for the

last round of the debate.

8. Spell:

Danny is going to his choir

_____ at seven

o'clock.

9. Spell:

Elephants, sheep, and cows are

_____ , which

means they feed on plants.

Spelling 6-10

10. Spell:

Jonathan could not _____ the story, so the carer had to explain it to him.

11. Spell:

Benjamin could _____ all his fears of height by traveling on the plane for the second time.

12. Spell:

The _____ of the box is ten centimeters long.

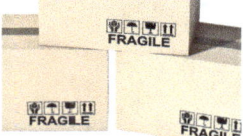

You completed lesson 10! Bravo! You are doing a great job. Very soon, you will be an expert in spelling.

Spelling 6-11

1. Spell:

Diana took a different _____ to school, which was faster for her.

2. Spell:

The team did not accept my _____ , so I stepped aside to hear others speak.

3. Spell:

The youth _____ meets on Sundays after church.

Spelling 6-11

4. Spell:
Lisa's father will be giving a talk at the Institute of _____ next month.

5. Spell:
The _____ guide has information about the town's history as well.

6. Spell:
The salesman got his expected _____ for selling the phones.

Spelling 6-11

7. Spell:
The doctor's _____ response saved him from a heart attack.

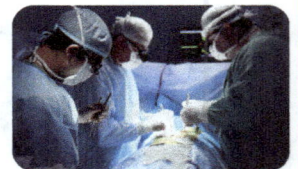

8. Spell:
Liam did request to discuss the issue with his _____ friend for clarity.

9. Spell:
The _____ of the school is quiet, serene, and friendly.

Spelling 6-11

10. Spell:

Joanna got a _____ job for the summer at the post office as a cashier.

11. Spell:

The clock on the wall is not _____, so don't depend on it for the correct time.

12. Spell:

The _____ building collapsed after the explosion.

You have finished the words in lesson 11. Fantastic!

Spelling 6-12

1. Spell:

The sick lady bore witness to the doctor's _____ when on duty.

2. Spell:

_____ was showing on Lima's face after the long jump exercise.

3. Spell:

He does not need a fence around his house because the trees' _____ is dense.

Spelling 6-12

4. Spell:

The town's _____ has increased to 500,000 people.

5. Spell:

There are _____ books that you can choose from in the library.

6. Spell:

Leo has been given an _____ to submit her homework.

Spelling 6-12

7. Spell:
The family _____ going from New York to Dubai for their holidays.

8. Spell:
Leo found it _____ to read the instruction manual before using his new phone.

9. Spell:
Davies and his friends were discussing their _____ during their free period.

Spelling 6-12

10. Spell:

Louie was eager to pick up Ella's

_____ call.

11. Spell:

Tina told the truth to keep a clean and

clear _____.

12. Spell:

Luke is a _____ pleasant, and

cheerful person to be with at

all times.

You have done excellent job finishing words in lesson 12. With this rhythm, you are about to be a master in spelling soon.

Spelling 6-13

1. Spell:
Ted is _____ with his equipment and tools.

2. Spell:
Sean's _____ made him ask several questions after the talk.

3. Spell:
Arthur _____ Liam to go to school despite his initial denial.

Spelling 6-13

4. Spell:

Dina is unsure _____ her mum or her dad will pick her up from school.

5. Spell:

Charlene got the _____ score on the exam and thrived among her classmates.

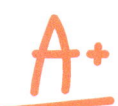

6. Spell:

Your village is one of the most _____ villages I have ever seen.

Spelling 6-13

7. Spell:

The doctor had to explain the _____ of things to Helen's dad so he could understand.

8. Spell:

David will _____ a new car for his 21st birthday.

9. Spell:

Jack listed his former teacher as a _____ for his holiday job.

Spelling 6-13

10. Spell:

The new equipment offered great

_____ to the

department.

11. Spell:

Anita had a _____ with her

daughter about finance.

12. Spell:

Jaden and Tina circled over the

_____ .

Congrats! You have made such Progress! You finished the words in lesson 13 already. Don't forget to practice new vocabulary every week. First, learn the meaning of the word, then the spelling of it. And then surprise everyone with your spelling skills.

Spelling 6-14

1. Spell:
George flew to London on a British Airways _____ for the first time.

2. Spell:
The _____ does not revolve around you, so don't be so egocentric.

3. Spell:
David stood on the _____ to discuss his issues with his mum.

Spelling 6-14

4. Spell:

Vaccination against _____ protects the elderly from death and lung health problems.

5. Spell:

Joe used his pocket money to repair his _____ phone.

6. Spell:

A _____ letter was sent from the bank to Mr. Smith.

Spelling 6-14

7. Spell:

The maths _____ is coming up on Friday.

8. Spell:

Mr. Scott is a man of _____ and true to his words.

9. Spell:

Cecelia's story was a _____ and interesting one.

Spelling 6-14

10. Spell:

Lion, tigers, and leopards are

_____ , which means

they feed on other animals.

11. Spell:

Many of the athletes in team three are

_____ and below

average.

12. Spell:

Thomson's boss is making his life

_____ because he

does not like him.

What progress! You completed lesson 14 already. You should be proud of yourself!

Spelling 6-15

1. Spell:

The _____ children were able to join in the sport day events.

2. Spell:

Sunday will be my parent's wedding _____ .

3. Spell:

The class is taking a tour of the British _____ on Friday after the break.

Spelling 6-15

4. Spell:

The science _____ was a huge success.

5. Spell:

Jayden called the _____ , and they arrived on time to save the pregnant lady.

6. Spell:

Betty has become a tennis _____ after several practices and won competitions.

Spelling 6-15

7. Spell:

They shook their hands and sealed the deal by signing an _____ .

8. Spell:

Doing your homework on time leaves you room for _____ time.

9. Spell:

The _____ cause of the pain was a headache.

Spelling 6-15

10. Spell:

Maria got a _____ feeling

when her mobile phone rang.

11. Spell:

Nancy is going to study at the college to

be an _____ .

12. Spell:

The community beach had a mix of

_____ and rough

sand.

Wonderful! You have completed words in lesson 15. Keep up the great work, and don't forget: words matter and most importantly, correctly written words matter.

Spelling 6-16

1. Spell:

All the guests were happy at the

_____ wedding.

2. Spell:

Cameron is tempted to _____ back for Joe's insult.

3. Spell:

Nick's mentor _____ him for being late in the session.

Spelling 6-16

4. Spell:

Mr. Yusuf can drive any kind of _____ as an experienced driver.

5. Spell:

Joshua and Jude were having a _____ over who will walk the dog.

6. Spell:

Amina is a frequent _____ to China and Japan, so she gets a ticket discount.

Spelling 6-16

7. Spell:

_____ , her name was not on the class register, so she could not participate.

8. Spell:

Mr. Liam had a conversation with Luke about his _____ spending.

9. Spell:

William's death was a terrible _____ for his family.

Spelling 6-16

10. Spell:

The director arranged a meeting for that _____ matter that came up in the department.

11. Spell:

Going on the coding course brought a _____ to Chloe.

12. Spell:

The raw materials used to _____ the plastics were obtained from China.

You're almost finished with becoming a spelling master. You are doing so well! You have completed words in spelling lesson 16. Bravo!

Spelling 6-17

1. Spell:

His workload has been reduced to a

_____ size.

2. Spell:

The coach was able to _____

the players before the game.

3. Spell:

Can you _____ Ashton

becoming a doctor?

Spelling 6-17

4. Spell:
Brook is not _____ to eat chocolate after dinner.

5. Spell:
Nicolas drew _____ lines in his book whenever he was bored.

6. Spell:
Suddenly, Mr. Marcus was told to _____ his car by his co-driver.

Spelling 6-17

7. Spell:

Jayden bought an _____ car for his wife, Sue.

8. Spell:

The author was able to _____ the story beautifully to engage the children.

9. Spell:

The teacher was _____ with the grades in the final test, so everyone passed.

Spelling 6-17

10. Spell:

Beau dropped out of the _____ because she was scared she would not win.

11. Spell:

Bilingual children that learn two _____ from their parents tend to be more clever.

12. Spell:

The new _____ is having a press conference at 3 o'clock today at the multipurpose building.

Fantastic! You have completed spelling lesson 17!

Spelling 6-18

1. Spell:

Lily wrote an _____ description of her maths teacher.

2. Spell:

Noah is having an _____ on Friday on his right eye.

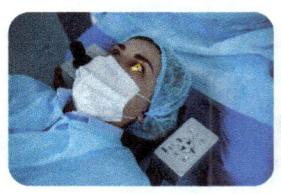

3. Spell:

I cherish all the _____ moments I had with my mentor.

Spelling 6-18

4. Spell:

Oliver's phone has a new

_____ that makes

it easier to text his messages.

5. Spell:

The hot food was nutritious and delicious,

which helped to _____

the body.

6. Spell:

The _____ drove the girls to

their prom.

Spelling 6-18

7. Spell:

A humidifier is a device that balances _____ in a room.

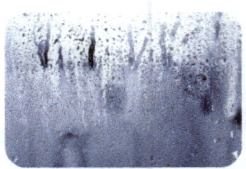

8. Spell:

Each printer has a _____ number on the back of it.

9. Spell:

She did not _____ and miss her deadline, so she submitted her work the same day.

Spelling 6-18

10. Spell:

The old lady went to his lawyer to

_____ her will to

leave everything for the charity.

11. Spell:

Harvey's experience has taught him to be

more _____

in trusting people.

12. Spell:

The _____ was good

because it brought in a new

era which is what is needed.

Spelling lesson 18 is over. You finished it and, more importantly, learned the lesson's words. However, if you have doubts about one or more words, do not worry; return to the word and make as many revisions as necessary.

Spelling 6-19

1. Spell:

David rode off at a _____ .

2. Spell:

_____ the day and try to make the most of it.

3. Spell:

The third room will be _____ next month when the tenant packs out.

Spelling 6-19

4. Spell:
The student _____ has called up the strike.

5. Spell:
Tyler did not want to _____ himself, so he did not sign the agreement.

6. Spell:
Fill in each _____ with the best answer.

Spelling 6-19

7. Spell:
It's_____! Tom and Jane are getting married next month.

8. Spell:
Daisy designed the _____ for the school play.

9. Spell:
The blue ball was floating on the _____ of the pool water.

Spelling 6-19

10. Spell:

Always be aware of where you put your

_____ .

11. Spell:

I am listening to my spelling dictation on

_____ .

12. Spell:

The socialist party has started to

_____ for the

next election.

Excellent work, kid! You have made it! Lesson 19 is complete.

Spelling 6-20

1. Spell:
The _____ spoke clearly and loudly to the audience about the message he had to deliver.

2. Spell:
The _____ on the ancient temple has worn out and cannot be read clearly.

3. Spell:
The word hear and here is a

_____ .

Spelling 6-20

4. Spell:

Long-term _____ can lead to depression.

5. Spell:

Crooks stayed all night making childcare _____ for his children when he travels at the weekend.

6. Spell:

Lexie's _____ cost her job because she wasn't doing her tasks on time.

Spelling 6-20

7. Spell:
The _____ of a cube is length multiplied by height multiplied by width.

8. Spell:
Ruby was _____ right with her suggestion.

9. Spell:
Chantel got her brief on her _____ .

Spelling 6-20

10. Spell:
Ella expressed her _____ to the bereaved family that lost a child in a car accident.

11. Spell:
Streets on Monday mornings are full of _____ .

12. Spell:
The labor party will _____ its fight against corruption with a law proposal.

Look how far you have gone by now. You have reached and completed lesson 20! What a student you are! Congratulations!

Spelling 6-21

1. Spell:

Siena acted as the play's main character and tried to _____ it in her summary.

2. Spell:

Mrs. Fox did _____ her favorite student to be the new head girl.

3. Spell:

Mr. Jackson gave _____ instructions to his class on how to play the game.

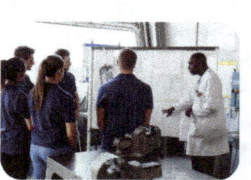

Spelling 6-21

4. Spell:

The documents sent to Susan's mum were

_____ .

5. Spell:

Frankie sang the song with her

_____ voice.

6. Spell:

Looking at the stars from the telescope

did _____ Tom.

Spelling 6-21

7. Spell:
Nick passed the _____ test, which gave him hope for the main one.

8. Spell:
Priscilla's teacher gave enough _____ on how to do the task.

9. Spell:
Nathaniel was welcomed _____ to the team by the coach.

Spelling 6-21

10. Spell:

The flight attendants did _____ what the passengers must do in an emergency.

11. Spell:

Oscar was the only one who solved the _____ of the lost treasure.

12. Spell:

It was not _____ for the pregnant lady to walk to the station alone.

You have completed lesson 21! Congratulations!

Spelling 6-22

1. Spell:

Diana's frequent visit to the toilet is

_____ during lessons.

2. Spell:

Tony is planning to _____ his engagement to Tina at the Christmas dinner.

3. Spell:

Dad went with mom for a weekend to Miami to celebrate their _____ anniversary.

Spelling 6-22

4. Spell:

Gracie was lying down on the

_____ grass to

relax.

5. Spell:

Phoebe canceled his hotel reservation, so

he had to _____

his initial deposit.

6. Spell:

Grandma's steak pie was crispy, hot, and

_____ .

Spelling 6-22

7. Spell:

Linsey did not have _____ money for a flight to France, so she went by train.

8. Spell:

Flynn was irritated with the _____ of her brother Aaron.

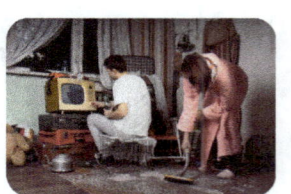

9. Spell:

Gilbert was asked not to _____ Mr. Greg when he was speaking.

Spelling 6-22

10. Spell:

Kieran got his information from a reliable

_____ online.

11. Spell:

Louisa will work as an _____

nurse from January at the

care home.

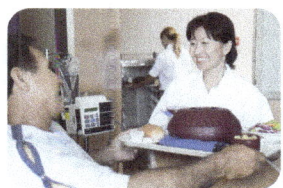

12. Spell:

Jones and Connelly fought a

_____ over the

new girl at their school.

Lesson 22 has come to an end. Awesome! Keep up the excellent work! And do not forget: Repetition makes the master.

Spelling 6-23

1. Spell:

Darcy found Elliot to be a good caring

_____ .

2. Spell:

Calvin ordered a new _____ from the shop to make his order.

3. Spell:

Clifford lost his costly _____ during the war.

Spelling 6-23

4. Spell:

What is your _____ on the subject?

5. Spell:

Johnson is respectful, obedient and respects his father's _____ over him.

6. Spell:

I have always wanted to _____ a zero-gravity flight.

Spelling 6-23

7. Spell:

It was easier to _____ the slide than to ascend on it.

8. Spell:

Lily-May will watch a new movie in the _____ on Friday after school.

9. Spell:

The two candidates for the President's position will have a _____ on T.V. tonight.

Spelling 6-23

10. Spell:

Evans came up with a _____ story that his parents did not believe.

11. Spell:

It took the firefighters about four minutes to _____ the fire in the camp.

12. Spell:

Gandhi was an Indian leader that could _____ millions of people.

Well done! You have finished lesson 23. You should be proud of yourself!

Spelling 6-24

1. Spell:
The new teacher helped Laura to understand the _____ of bony fishes.

2. Spell:
Calvin is thinking of being a data analyst as his future _____ .

3. Spell:
Ted wasted the _____ time he could have used to revise for his exam.

Spelling 6-24

4. Spell:

Harrison cooked the chicken curry _____ for his mum though his dad had some.

5. Spell:

The Board of Directions decided on the _____ of the company's stocks.

6. Spell:

Jamie was able to _____ his parents with his drama performance.

Spelling 6-24

7. Spell:

Having a _____ glued on the fridge's door helps us program our shopping better.

8. Spell:

The movie attracted a large _____ worldwide. It has been a blockbuster!

9. Spell:

Please don't _____ the music recording.

Spelling 6-24

10. Spell:

Mr. Kelly will have to _____ Robert and Ronnie to a different class.

11. Spell:

There was a _____ of fruits to choose from at the hotel's breakfast buffet.

12. Spell:

Scott and Andrew had to write a _____ statement as they were there at the accident scene.

Great! Lesson 24 is over! I suggest you get some rest before going on to the next lesson. That will help you recharge and return to the next task more refreshed! Great work!

Spelling 6-25

1. Spell:
Ryan had the _____ of schooling in a private boarding house where he learned coding.

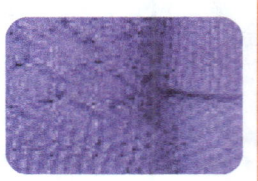

2. Spell:
Maisie threw heavy purple _____ clothes on her daughter's shoulder.

3. Spell:
The caterer came up with a _____ price for preparing all the meals.

Spelling 6-25

4. Spell:

Dulcie lost her _____ when she saw how the food was prepared.

5. Spell:

Hassan laughed as the _____ made the doll speak loudly without moving it's lips.

6. Spell:

The school _____ has appointed a new Spanish teacher for the next academic year.

Spelling 6-25

7. Spell:

Bullying can be a form of _____ abuse.

8. Spell:

Archie was able to _____ two different colors for his art collage.

9. Spell:

Rose could feel a tiny little _____ moving on her leg.

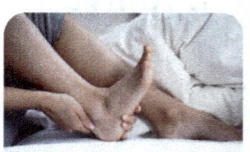

Spelling 6-25

10. Spell:

Harvey's _____ has taught him to be more cautious in trusting people.

11. Spell:

The revolution was good because it _____ a new era with more freedom and rights for people.

12. Spell:

_____ his country at the Olympic Games made him very proud.

Here we are! Last lesson, and you have reached the end of Spelling 6. Do you feel like you have conquered the vocabulary and spelling field? Great! You should be proud of yourself. If, however, you do not feel very confident with some of the words, repeat them again and again until you fully understand the meaning and the orthography.

Conclusion

Hurray! You have made it! You have just arrived at the end of Spelling 6. Bravo!

Now give yourself a round of applause for getting this far. You deserve it, and you must be proud of yourself. I am proud of you!

Hopefully, you have added 300 new words to your vocabulary, making your spelling skills more acute and your memory stronger.

That is to say that you have just gained an asset. How does it feel to get ahead of your peers and classmates?

I guess it feels nice. And don't worry if you missed some of the words. Repetition makes perfect, so take the book from the start and persist with the words that gave you a difficult time while studying. You can master the words by repeating them five times.

The next appointment is Spelling 7. I'll meet you there.

Please leave a 1-click Review!

I would be incredibly thankful if you could take just 60 seconds to write a brief review on Amazon or the platform of purchase, even if it's just a few sentences!

Sneak Peak!

I would like to share with you a sneak peek into one of my other audiobooks that I think you would really enjoy.

The audiobook is called "Spelling Seven: An Interactive Vocabulary & Spelling Workbook for 12-14 Years Olds" and it is a spelling book that covers words every teen must know and are frequently misspelled in exams. It is broken down into easy-to-follow spelling exercises that take only 10 minutes per day.

Hope you enjoy this free chapter!

Spelling 7-1

1. Spell:

Benedict was able to behave herself in her teacher's _____ .

2. Spell:

The opponents tried hard to _____ the team but they were united in their goal.

3. Spell:

Freya launched into a furious _____ because of how she had been treated.

Spelling 7-1

4. Spell:

Benedicta is a decent lady of

_____ gesture.

5. Spell:

Shooters escorted the _____

as he stepped out of the plane.

6. Spell:

All of the money was kept in the bank's

_____ .

Spelling 7-1

7. Spell:

The British Airways plane _____ down the runway.

8. Spell:

The homework was not _____, so Katie had to do it again.

9. Spell:

Davies was hungry, and he _____ all the food on his plate.

Spelling 7-1

10. Spell:

Thomas _____ all his information and data from various sources.

11. Spell:

Emily's father _____ the idea that she was old enough to set her curfews.

12. Spell:

You do not need to be a _____ to see that Chloe and John's plan will not work.

You've done it! You completed lesson 1.

Spelling 7-2

1. Spell:

The _____ stood to sing a hymn for the church's Sunday worship.

2. Spell:

The cashier checked that the signature on the cheque was an _____ one.

3. Spell:

Molly was angry with Jackson for trying to _____ her.

Spelling 7-2

4. Spell:

The government had to impose a twenty-four-hour _____ throughout the state.

5. Spell:

Harry was _____ about his opinion and refused to listen to no one else.

6. Spell:

Orchard was happy and delighted to _____ Cooper in his house.

Spelling 7-2

7. Spell:

Richard did not type in the

partial partial partial partial PIN, so he

could not withdraw his money.

8. Spell:

Charles was able to _partial partial partial partial_

level eight in his swimming with

much practice.

9. Spell:

Caitlin watched the snake

partial partial partial partial across the

garden.

Spelling 7-2

10. Spell:

The French _____ that killed a lot of people was bloody.

11. Spell:

Scott put out a lot of _____ on his first point in his argument.

12. Spell:

Mia _____ the data and was able to use it for her presentation.

Well done for completing lesson 2!

Spelling 7-3

1. Spell:
An _____ is someone who lacks basic literacy and numeracy skills.

2. Spell:
Allen saw _____ faces looking through the window to see what he would do.

3. Spell:
Joe _____ to be a teacher but has changed his mind.

Spelling 7-3

4. Spell:

Camron was humble enough to _____ his fault in making the wrong calculations.

5. Spell:

Dennis is an _____ boy.

6. Spell:

The _____ had ten fishes in it.

Spelling 7-3

7. Spell:
The south-End beach was _____ with teenagers on Saturday.

8. Spell:
Tim has been working hard on his _____, which is due tomorrow.

9. Spell:
Bobby is a _____ child.

Spelling 7-3

10. Spell:

Skye is a racist _____ ; she does not like to speak to anyone who is not her race.

11. Spell:

Isla broke the curfew and, _____ , did not have her phone for two weeks.

12. Spell:

Mr. Bradley made some_____ changes to his house, selling it at a higher price.

Well done for completing lesson 3!

Spelling 7-4

1. Spell:

The _____ predicted a mild rain the next day.

2. Spell:

Millie is considering changing her _____ from a teacher to a study coach.

3. Spell:

Callum was authorized to look into the _____ number of complaints he received.

Spelling 7-4

4. Spell:

Sofia spent her _____ career in one school.

5. Spell:

Mobile phones have become an _____ part of human life.

6. Spell:

Archie tried hard to act _____ , but his eyes were full of mischief.

Spelling 7-4

7. Spell:

An _____ view of Sydney

shows how beautiful it is.

8. Spell:

Riley has never flown on an

_____ before.

9. Spell:

George was quite _____

with the new plan.

Spelling 7-4

10. Spell:

Lennie could read and write wholly but decently _____.

11. Spell:

It was unkind of Abigail to _____ Luke's level 9 achievement.

12. Spell:

Billy saw the mouse trying to _____ under the door.

You've made it! You completed lesson 4.

Spelling 7-5

1. Spell:

Nathan tried hard not to _____ the truth when asked questions on politics.

2. Spell:

Lennie wrote a _____ letter to the school about her health.

3. Spell:

Ella did not have Tony's email _____ , so she could not contact him during the summer.

Spelling 7-5

4. Spell:

Lois went to _____ Betsy if she would come along with her for a stroll to the mall.

5. Spell:

Madison asked the lab _____ for help with her experiment.

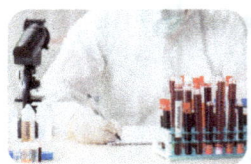

6. Spell:

Jacob ceased to be a member of the _____.

Spelling 7-5

7. Spell:

Harris is the best _____ in his school.

8. Spell:

Connie ought not to have brought up the old _____ that she brought up.

9. Spell:

Harry has had sleep _____ which is resulting in his disorderliness.

Spelling 7-5

10. Spell:

Alan drew a symbol to represent an Egyptian _____ in his artwork.

11. Spell:

Smith seems to have so much _____ towards Thomas.

12. Spell:

Alex offered his _____ to Logan for being re-elected as the team leader.

You have done excellent job finishing words in lesson 5.

Answers

Spelling 6-1

1. Spell: <u>Submit</u>
2. Spell: <u>Curious</u>
3. Spell: <u>Humor (US)</u>
   <u>Humour (UK)</u>
4. Spell: <u>Electricity</u>
5. Spell: <u>Biography</u>
6. Spell: <u>Bachelor</u>
7. Spell: <u>Ache</u>
8. Spell: <u>Enroll (US)</u>
   <u>Enrol (UK)</u>
9. Spell: <u>Fraud</u>
10. Spell: <u>Muscle</u>
11. Spell: <u>Labor (US)</u>
    <u>Labour (UK)</u>
12. Spell: <u>Condemn</u>

Spelling 6-2

1. Spell: <u>Guilty</u>
2. Spell: <u>Disease</u>
3. Spell: <u>Occur</u>
4. Spell: <u>Credit</u>
5. Spell: <u>Superior</u>
6. Spell: <u>Imitate</u>
7. Spell: <u>Conversation</u>
8. Spell: <u>Stationary</u>
9. Spell: <u>Pedestal</u>
10. Spell: <u>Literate</u>
11. Spell: <u>Rumor (US)</u>
    <u>Rumour (UK)</u>
12. Spell: <u>Testimony</u>

Answers

Spelling 6-3

1. Spell: Yield
2. Spell: Desire
3. Spell: Mayor
4. Spell: Period
5. Spell: Extreme
6. Spell: Foreign
7. Spell: Misspelled
8. Spell: Oblige
9. Spell: Influence
10. Spell: Education
11. Spell: Comparison
12. Spell: Sealing

Spelling 6-4

1. Spell: Delicious
2. Spell: Encircle
3. Spell: Kerosene
4. Spell: Community
5. Spell: Emergency
6. Spell: Invisible
7. Spell: Reduce
8. Spell: Museum
9. Spell: Exhaust
10. Spell: Plumber
11. Spell: Equinox
12. Spell: Pedestrian

Answers

Spelling 6-5

1. Spell: <u>Suffix</u>
2. Spell: <u>Inhabitant</u>
3. Spell: <u>Satisfactory</u>
4. Spell: <u>Aisle</u>
5. Spell: <u>Innocent</u>
6. Spell: <u>Genuine</u>
7. Spell: <u>Salute</u>
8. Spell: <u>Pursue</u>
9. Spell: <u>Realize (US)</u>
   <u>Realise (UK)</u>
10. Spell: <u>Vacuum</u>
11. Spell: <u>Severe</u>
12. Spell: <u>Provision</u>

Spelling 6-6

1. Spell: <u>Gradual</u>
2. Spell: <u>Squash</u>
3. Spell: <u>Smoky</u>
4. Spell: <u>Territory</u>
5. Spell: <u>Theory</u>
6. Spell: <u>Siege</u>
7. Spell: <u>Feint</u>
8. Spell: <u>Minority</u>
9. Spell: <u>Deposit</u>
10. Spell: <u>Ignorant</u>
11. Spell: <u>Sufficient</u>
12. Spell: <u>Region</u>

Answers

Spelling 6-7

1. Spell: Condition
2. Spell: Ceiling
3. Spell: League
4. Spell: Cease
5. Spell: Motion
6. Spell: Gauge
7. Spell: Justify
8. Spell: Gallery
9. Spell: Essay
10. Spell: Recognize (US) Recognise (UK)
11. Spell: Insolent
12. Spell: Particle

Spelling 6-8

1. Spell: Loathe
2. Spell: Influence
3. Spell: Starvation
4. Spell: Deceive
5. Spell: Elastic
6. Spell: Movable
7. Spell: Average
8. Spell: Popular
9. Spell: Political
10. Spell: Permanent
11. Spell: Appreciate
12. Spell: Official

Answers

Spelling 6-9

1. Spell: <u>Adventurous</u>
2. Spell: <u>Imagination</u>
3. Spell: <u>Cassette</u>
4. Spell: <u>Barren</u>
5. Spell: <u>Mischievous</u>
6. Spell: <u>Soprano</u>
7. Spell: <u>Bouquet</u>
8. Spell: <u>Occasion</u>
9. Spell: <u>Insurance</u>
10. Spell: <u>Spirit</u>
11. Spell: <u>Fiction</u>
12. Spell: <u>Frequent</u>

Spelling 6-10

1. Spell: <u>Apology</u>
2. Spell: <u>Preserve</u>
3. Spell: <u>Sergeant</u>
4. Spell: <u>Success</u>
5. Spell: <u>Peace</u>
6. Spell: <u>Preparation</u>
7. Spell: <u>Strength</u>
8. Spell: <u>Practise (US)</u> <u>Practice (UK)</u>
9. Spell: <u>Herbivorous</u>
10. Spell: <u>Comprehend</u>
11. Spell: <u>Vanquish</u>
12. Spell: <u>Width</u>

Answers

Spelling 6-11

1. Spell: Route
2. Spell: Opinion
3. Spell: Association
4. Spell: Taxation
5. Spell: Tourist
6. Spell: Commission
7. Spell: Immediate
8. Spell: Intimate
9. Spell: Atmosphere
10. Spell: Temporary
11. Spell: Reliable
12. Spell: Entire

Spelling 6-12

1. Spell: Patience
2. Spell: Fatigue
3. Spell: Foliage
4. Spell: Population
5. Spell: Numerous
6. Spell: Extension
7. Spell: Preferred
8. Spell: Necessary
9. Spell: Religion
10. Spell: Telephone
11. Spell: Conscience
12. Spell: Friendly

Answers

Spelling 6-13

1. Spell: <u>Clumsy</u>
2. Spell: <u>Curiosity</u>
3. Spell: <u>Persuaded</u>
4. Spell: <u>Whether</u>
5. Spell: <u>Maximum</u>
6. Spell: <u>Picturesque</u>
7. Spell: <u>Situation</u>
8. Spell: <u>Purchase</u>
9. Spell: <u>Reference</u>
10. Spell: <u>Assistance</u>
11. Spell: <u>Discussion</u>
12. Spell: <u>Aerodrome</u>

Spelling 6-14

1. Spell: <u>Aeroplane</u>
2. Spell: <u>Universe</u>
3. Spell: <u>Veranda</u>
4. Spell: <u>Influenza</u>
5. Spell: <u>Faulty</u>
6. Spell: <u>Confidential</u>
7. Spell: <u>Assessment</u>
8. Spell: <u>Principle</u>
9. Spell: <u>Credible</u>
10. Spell: <u>Carnivorous</u>
11. Spell: <u>Mediocre</u>
12. Spell: <u>Miserable</u>

Answers

Spelling 6-15

1. Spell: Handicapped
2. Spell: Anniversary
3. Spell: Parliament
4. Spell: Experiment
5. Spell: Ambulance
6. Spell: Champion
7. Spell: Agreement
8. Spell: Leisure
9. Spell: Probable
10. Spell: Peculiar
11. Spell: Architect
12. Spell: Coarse

Spelling 6-16

1. Spell: Magnificent
2. Spell: Retaliate
3. Spell: Reprimanded
4. Spell: Vehicle
5. Spell: Squabble
6. Spell: Traveler (US) Traveller (UK)
7. Spell: Apparently
8. Spell: Wasteful
9. Spell: Tragedy
10. Spell: Serious
11. Spell: Benefit
12. Spell: Manufacture

Answers

Spelling 6-17

1. Spell: Manageable
2. Spell: Encourage
3. Spell: Imagine
4. Spell: Allowed
5. Spell: Straight
6. Spell: Accelerate
7. Spell: Expensive
8. Spell: Illustrate
9. Spell Favorable (US) Favourable (UK)
10. Spell: Competition
11. Spell: Languages
12. Spell: Minister

Spelling 6-18

1. Spell: Excellent
2. Spell: Operation
3. Spell: Precious
4. Spell: Feature
5. Spell: Nourish
6. Spell: Chauffeur
7. Spell: Humidity
8. Spell: Serial
9. Spell: Procrastinate
10. Spell: Alter
11. Spell: Cautious
12. Spell: Revolution

Answers

Spelling 6-19

1. Spell: Gallop
2. Spell: Seize
3. Spell: Vacant
4. Spell: Union
5. Spell: Commit
6. Spell: Column
7. Spell: Official
8. Spell: Scenery
9. Spell: Surface
10. Spell: Signature
11. Spell: Audible
12. Spell: Campaign

Spelling 6-20

1. Spell: Prophet
2. Spell: Inscription
3. Spell: Homophone
4. Spell: Loneliness
5. Spell: Arrangement
6. Spell: Laziness
7. Spell: Volume
8. Spell: Probably
9. Spell: Telegram
10. Spell: Sympathy
11. Spell: Traffic
12. Spell: Intensify

Answers

Spelling 6-21

1. Spell: Magnify
2. Spell: Recommend
3. Spell: Specific
4. Spell: Confidential
5. Spell: Masculine
6. Spell: Fascinate
7. Spell: Preliminary
8. Spell: Information
9. Spell: Cordially
10. Spell: Illustrate
11. Spell: Mystery
12. Spell: Convenient

Spelling 6-22

1. Spell: Suspicious
2. Spell: Announce
3. Spell: Twelfth
4. Spell: Artificial
5. Spell: Forfeit
6. Spell: Delicious
7. Spell: Sufficient
8. Spell: Slovenly
9. Spell: Interrupt
10. Spell: Source
11. Spell: Auxiliary
12. Spell: Duel

Answers

Spelling 6-23

1. Spell: Companion
2. Spell: Catalog (US) Catalogue (UK)
3. Spell: Possession
4. Spell: Opinion
5. Spell: Authority
6. Spell: Experience
7. Spell: Descend
8. Spell: Theatre
9. Spell: Debate
10. Spell: Plausible
11. Spell: Extinguish
12. Spell: Influence

Spelling 6-24

1. Spell: Classification
2. Spell: Career
3. Spell: Precious
4. Spell: Especially
5. Spell: Allotment
6. Spell: Astonish
7. Spell: Calendar
8. Spell: Audience
9. Spell: Interrupt
10. Spell: Transfer
11. Spell: Variety
12. Spell: Witness

Answers

Spelling 6-25

1. Spell: Advantage
2. Spell: Woolen (US)
   Wollen (UK)
3. Spell: Ridiculous
4. Spell: Appetite
5. Spell: Ventriloquist
6. Spell: Council
7. Spell: Physical
8. Spell: Combine
9. Spell Creature
10. Spell: Experience
11. Spell: Brought
12. Spell: Representing

Spelling 7-1

1. Spell: Absence
2. Spell: Demoralize (US)
   Demoralise (UK)
3. Spell: Tirade
4. Spell: Magnanimous
5. Spell: Fugitive
6. Spell: Vault
7. Spell: Accelerated
8. Spell: Acceptable
9. Spell: Devoured
10. Spell: Gleaned
11. Spell: Dissented
12. Spell: Genius

Answers

Spelling 7-2

1. Spell: Congregation
2. Spell: Authentic
3. Spell: Delude
4. Spell: Curfew
5. Spell: Adamant
6. Spell: Accommodate
7. Spell: Accurate
8. Spell: Achieve
9. Spell Slither
10. Spell: Massacre
11. Spell: Emphasis
12. Spell: Analyzed (US) Analysed (UK)

Spelling 7-3

1. Spell: Illiterate
2. Spell: Inquisitive
3. Spell: Aspired
4. Spell: Acknowledge
5. Spell: Independent
6. Spell: Aquarium
7. Spell: Teeming
8. Spell: Assignment
9. Spell: Precocious
10. Spell: Bigot
11. Spell: Consequently
12. Spell: Cosmetic

Answers

Spelling 7-4

1. Spell: <u>Meteorologist</u>
2. Spell: <u>Occupation</u>
3. Spell: <u>Considerable</u>
4. Spell: <u>Academic</u>
5. Spell: <u>Indispensable</u>
6. Spell: <u>Innocent</u>
7. Spell: <u>Aerial</u>
8. Spell: <u>Aeroplane</u>
9. Spell <u>Agreeable</u>
10. Spell: <u>Innumerate</u>
11. Spell: <u>Denigrate</u>
12. Spell: <u>Scurry</u>

Spelling 7-5

1. Spell: <u>Evade</u>
2. Spell: <u>Confidential</u>
3. Spell: <u>Address</u>
4. Spell: <u>Ask</u>
5. Spell: <u>Assistant</u>
6. Spell: <u>Association</u>
7. Spell: <u>Athlete</u>
8. Spell: <u>Reminiscence</u>
9. Spell: <u>Deprivation</u>
10. Spell: <u>Deity</u>
11. Spell: <u>Animosity</u>
12. Spell: <u>Congratulations</u>

Other Books You'll Love!

1. **Spelling one: An Interactive Vocabulary & Spelling** Workbook for 5-Year-Olds. (With Audiobook Lessons)

2. **Spelling Two: An Interactive Vocabulary & Spelling** Workbook for 6-Year-Olds. (With Audiobook Lessons)

3. **Spelling Three: An Interactive Vocabulary & Spelling** Workbook for 7-Year-Olds. (With Audiobook Lessons)

4. **Spelling Four: An Interactive Vocabulary & Spelling** Workbook for 8-Year-Olds. (With Audiobook Lessons)

5. **Spelling Five: An Interactive Vocabulary & Spelling** Workbook for 9-Year-Olds. (With Audiobook Lessons)

6. **Spelling Six: An Interactive Vocabulary & Spelling** Workbook for 10 & 11 Years Old. (With Audiobook Lessons)

7. **Spelling Seven: An Interactive Vocabulary & Spelling** Workbook for 12-14 Years-Old. (With Audiobook Lessons)

Other Books You'll Love!

8. **Raising Boys in Today's Digital World:**
Proven Positive Parenting Tips for Raising Respectful, Successful, and Confident Boys

9. **Raising Girls in Today's Digital World:**
Proven Positive Parenting Tips for Raising Respectful, Successful, and Confident Girls

10. **Raising Kids in Today's Digital World:**
Proven Positive Parenting Tips for Raising Respectful, Successful, and Confident Kids

11. **The Child Development and Positive Parenting Master Class 2-in-1 Bundle:**
Proven Methods for Raising Well-Behaved and Intelligent Children, with Accelerated Learning Methods

12. **Parenting Teens in Today's Challenging World 2-in-1 Bundle:** Proven Methods for Improving Teenager's Behaviour with Positive Parenting and Family Communication

13. **Life Strategies for Teenagers:**
Positive Parenting, Tips and Understanding Teens for Better Communication and a Happy Family

14. **Parenting Teen Girls in Today's Challenging World:**
Proven Methods for Improving Teenager's Behaviour with Whole Brain Training

Other Books You'll Love!

15. **Parenting Teen Boys in Today's Challenging World:**
Proven Methods for Improving Teenager's Behaviour with Whole Brain Training

16. **101 Tips For Helping With Your Child's Learning**:
Proven Strategies for Accelerated Learning and Raising Smart Children Using Positive Parenting Skills

17. **101 Tips for Child Development:**
Proven Methods for Raising Children and Improving Kids Behavior with Whole Brain Training

18. **Financial Tips to Help Kids:**
Proven Methods for Teaching Kids Money Management and Financial Responsibility

19. **Healthy Habits for Kids:**
Positive Parenting Tips for Fun Kids Exercises, Healthy Snacks, and Improved Kids Nutrition

20. **Mini Habits for Happy Kids:**
Proven Parenting Tips for Positive Discipline and Improving Kids' Behavior

21. **Good Habits for Healthy Kids 2-in-1 Combo Pack**:
Proven Positive Parenting Tips for Improving Kid's Fitness and Children's Behavior

Other Books You'll Love!

22. Raising Teenagers to Choose Wisely:
Keeping your Teen Secure in a Big World

23. Tips for #CollegeLife:
Powerful College Advice for Excelling as a College Freshman

24 The Career Success Formula:
Proven Career Development Advice and Finding Rewarding Employment for Young Adults and College Graduates

25. The Motivated Young Adult's Guide to Career Success and Adulthood:
Proven Tips for Becoming a Mature Adult, Starting a Rewarding Career, and Finding Life Balance

26. Bedtime Stories for Kids:
Short Funny Stories and poems Collection for Children and Toddlers

27. Guide for Boarding School Life

28. The Fear of The Lord:
How God's Honour Guarantees Your Peace

Audiobooks

Are available at any of the following retailers:

1. Kobo
https://www.kobo.com/us/en/audiobook/spelling-six

2. Google Store
https://play.google.com/store/audiobooks/details/Bukky_Ekine_Ogunlana_Spelling_Six?id=AQAAAECiFABUsM

3. Libro
https://libro.fm/audiobooks/9798368943251

4. Storytel
https://www.storytel.com/se/sv/books/4308271-Spelling-Six-An-Interactive-Vocabulary-and-Spelling-Workbook-for-10-and-11-Years-Old-With-Audiobook-Lessons

5. Scribd/Everbrand
https://www.everand.com/audiobook/642026064/Spelling-Six-An-Interactive-Vocabulary-and-Spelling-Workbook-for-10-and-11-Years-Old-With-Audiobook-Lessons

6. Barnes and Noble
https://www.audiobooks.co.uk/audiobook/spelling-six-an-interactive-vocabulary-and-spelling-workbook-for-10-and-11-years-old-with-audiobook-lessons/684460

7. Spotify
https://open.spotify.com/show/4ExDlbP399EOh7Jt1oLbjX

8. Chirpbooks
https://www.chirpbooks.com/audiobooks/spelling-six-by-bukky-ekine-ogunlana

And all other audiobook retailers!

Your Free Gift

Your Free Gift!

As a way of saying thank you for Your purchase, I have included a gift that you can download at

TCECpublishing.com

Facebook Community

I invite you to our Facebook community group to visit this link and simply click the join group.

https://www.facebook.com/groups/397683731371863

This is a private group where parents, teachers, and carers can learn, share tips, ask questions, and discuss and get valuable content about raising and parenting modern children.

It is a very supportive and encouraging group where valuable content, free resources, and exciting discussion about parenting are shared. You can use this to benefit from social media.

You will learn a lot from schoolteachers, experts, counselors, and new and experienced parents, and stay updated with our latest releases.

See you there!

References

[1] https://www.theseus.fi/bitstream/handle/10024/50239/Anttila_Marianna_Saikkonen_Pinja.pdf

[2] https://www.researchgate.net/publication/283721084_Early_Reading_Development

[3] https://www2.ed.gov/parents/academic/help/adolescence/adolescence.pdf

[4] http://centerforchildwelfare.org/kb/prprouthome/Helping%20Your%20Children%20Navigate%20Their%20Teenage%20Years.pdf

[5] https://www.childrensmn.org/images/family_resource_pdf/027121.pdf

[6] https://educationnorthwest.org/sites/default/files/developing-empathy-in-children--and-youth.pdf

[7] https://www.researchgate.net/publication/263227023_Family_Time_Activities_and_Adolescents'_Emotional_Well-being

[8] http://www.delmarlearning.com/companions/content/1418019224/Additional_Support/box11.1.pdf

[9] https://exeter.anglican.org/wp-content/uploads/2014/11/Listening-to-children-leaflet_NCB.pdf

[10] https://www.researchgate.net/publication/312600262_Creative_Thinking_among_Preschool_Children

www.ingramcontent.com/pod-product-compliance
Lightning Source LLC
Chambersburg PA
CBHW050028130526
44590CB00042B/2183